YOUNG CITIZEN...

IN THE STREET

Kate Brookes

WAYLAND

Other titles in the series
At Home
At School
Growing Up

Editor: Sarah Doughty
Photostylist: Gina Brown
Specially commissioned photographs: Pat and Charles
Aithie/Ffotograff.
Designer: Simon Borrough
Illustrator: Mike Flanagan

This edition published in 2000 by
Wayland Publishers Ltd
61 Western Road, Hove
East Sussex BN3 1JD

British Library Cataloguing in Publication Data
Brookes, Kate
        In the Street. – (Young Citizen)
        1. Ethics – Juvenile Literature
        I. Title
        170

ISBN 0 7502 2345 6

Printed and bound by EuroGrafica S.p.A., Italy

find Wayland on the Internet at http://www.wayland.co.uk

CONTENTS

It's your choice	4
What time do you call this?	6
You've got to have a plan	8
It's not fair!	10
Getting on with the neighbours	12
Wheely good times	14
Mind your manners	16
I was so embarrassed!	18
Feeling under pressure	20
Keep away! Danger zones!	22
The fun zones	24
What if something happens?	26
The big quiz	28
Glossary	30
Books to read/useful contacts	31
Index	32

It's Your choice

It doesn't matter whether you're tossing a ball outside your home, chatting with friends on the corner of your street or out and about on your own. There are choices to be made. You can choose to go out and have a good time, a bad time or a downright dangerous time. What choice will you make?

Here's Daniel's story. He's not allowed out alone but when his older friends ask him to come to their den, he can't resist.

DANIEL INTO THE DEN

It's so boring at home. I wish Mum would let me go out alone.

Dan, want to come to the den?

Hey, it's Dan the Man.

You bet!

Race you there.

I won't tell Mum. The den's only down the road.

Last one's a rotten egg!

Oh, help!

Stupid kid just ran out on the road without even looking. I could have killed him.

What things did Daniel forget to do?

Why isn't he allowed out alone?

Is his Mum too strict?

Did his older friends set him a good example?

Do you know how to cross the road safely?

4

STOP, LOOK, READ THIS

Who's your choice for 'Best Dressed'?

Knowing where and when it's safest to cross a road is not just about being 'old enough'. There's loads of things to consider: How fast is the traffic moving? Which direction is it coming from? Where's the traffic going to? Is the road slippery? Can the drivers see you? Can you see what's coming? Tricky stuff indeed for people of any age.

WHAT DOES IT MEAN TO HAVE CHOICES?

When you start walking or catching the bus to school, doing errands or visiting your friends, you're being trusted and given responsibility. It's a big change! Even just going to the corner shop involves lots of decisions. You can decide to come back on time or be late, buy things you're not allowed to buy, take a short cut through a lonely wood, cross against the lights or chat to a stranger.

Good decisions will mean that you will have a chance to make more good choices. Bad decisions could lead to trouble. Has Becky and her friends made good or bad decisions?

"It's great fun upsetting the oldies. It's a real laugh to see their faces when they open the door to see who's knocked and nobody's there." **Beccy**

"We were having so much fun, we lost track of the time. Our parents went ballistic when we finally got home. I don't know why we didn't phone them." **David and Gerald**

"If I go where I say I'm going, come home at the right time and everything, my Dad knows he can trust me." **Abigail**

"I'm only allowed to play near home, but if I want to go to my friend's house I ask my Mum first." **Nicholas**

"I love going out with my big brother. He and his mates do really fun things together. Dad knows I'm safe." **Harry**

WHAT TIME DO YOU CALL THIS?

Want to know why things can get so stressy as you get older? Well, listen carefully. First, there's you wanting to be more responsible for what you do, when you do it and where you go. Then there's your parents and other adults, who want to be sure that you're up to the job of looking after yourself and being more independent.

Can you see why there's hassle? While you're trying to convince everyone you're ready for some independence, everyone is worrying if you really are. So, how can this be sorted out?

1. Put yourself in your parents' shoes so that you can understand their fears. Newspapers, radio and television are full of very sad stories about children and teenagers and crime on the streets.

2. Don't shout and mope about 'how they treat you like a baby' as this convinces adults that you're not ready. Instead, try calmly talking about it.

4. Don't ask for the Moon, when all you really want is to play outside your home, walk to school, go to the shop or visit a nearby friend's house. Take it one step at a time.

3. Agree on some rules about where you can go, what time you must be back, who you can go with and what you can do.

5. Stick to the rules to show that you're responsible, careful and considerate. One day, the Moon will be yours!

THE BIG QUESTIONS

When you're not allowed to do something or go somewhere, is your parent being strict, concerned or over-protective?

If you come home later than agreed, what do you think will happen?

HOW DOES IT FEEL?

If you let a parent down by breaking the rules about going out, you're also doing yourself no favours. Do this quiz to find out how it feels to be disappointed. You can choose as many answers as you like for each question.

1. Your best friend says she'll walk to school with you. How do you feel when she turns up very late?
a) Annoyed.
b) Upset.
c) Worried.

2. You get permission to go to the library with a friend, but your friend's real destination is the park. Is your friend ...
a) Dishonest?
b) Unreliable?
c) Going to get you into trouble?

3. A friend tells his parent that he is at your house, when he's gone somewhere else. What do you think about this?
a) It's dangerous. If something happens, no one will know where he is.
b) If your friend lies about this, what else does he lie about?
c) He's not the best sort of friend to have.

4. Your Mum says that she will collect you from swimming, but she doesn't turn up. What do you say to her?
a) I can't trust you.
b) You let me down and I was worried.
c) You're grounded for one week!

If you want to go out alone or with friends, then you and your friends have to tell your parents what the plans are. Nothing spooks parents more than not knowing what's going on. You like to know what your parents are up to, don't you?

This is what you've got to do:

1. Get organized: who's going, where you're going, what you're doing, what time it's happening, how you're getting there and back.

2. Make sure each parent gets the same story.

3. If plans have to change, then let everyone know.

4. Don't get involved in any lies about what's happening.

Don't leave home without ...

Knowing how you're getting home.

Money.

Phone card.

ID card with your name, address, phone number and medical information.

Useful telephone numbers.

Telling someone where you're going and leaving contact names and telephone numbers.

If you don't get this right, then this is what happens ...

A GREAT DAY OUT – NOT!

The cinema, that's a great idea.

How will you all get there and back?

OK, see you tomorrow.

1

So what's the arrangement? Do you want me to pick you up?

No, it's all sorted.

Are you sure?

I said it's sorted, didn't I?

2

It's not fair!

Everyone's parents are different and each will allow their children different amounts of freedom. Just because you're allowed to do something, it doesn't mean that your friend will be allowed to do it, too.

What you can and can't do, and where you can and can't go depends on where you live and your family's cultural background and beliefs. Some parents are very protective. This means that they don't allow their children to go out alone or to go to certain places.

You and your friends may be the same age, but everyone develops differently. There may be some things that you're ready to do, that your best friend isn't.

If you force a friend to do something they don't want to do, it's called peer pressure. Peer pressure has nothing to do with being a good friend. There's more about peer pressure on page 20.

The best of friends

Here is what some friends say:

"I'm not allowed to go out much. My brother once got into trouble and my Dad's never let us forget it. The kids at school call me a 'baby' when I say I can't go somewhere. Suki understands and she sticks by me." **Katrina**

"Katrina's Dad is strict but he knows he can trust me. He would let Katrina come to a party as long as I went with her. I wouldn't do anything to hurt our friendship." **Suki**

"I don't have much money, so when my friends wanted to go bowling or to the cinema, I always told them I was busy. I only told Courtney the real reason as she's my best mate." **Joel**

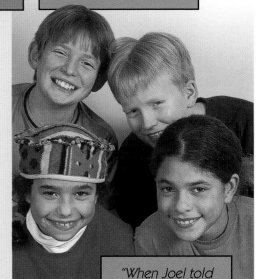

"My family is very religious and there are things I can't do. The kids at school think it's strange. The only one who's made an effort to understand is Sabrina." **Gunraj**

"Just because Gunraj follows his religion it doesn't mean that he can't do anything. Once I knew what was OK and what was not, there was still heaps we could do. We have lots of fun together and are good mates." **Sabrina**

"When Joel told me why he couldn't go out with us, I decided that we must do things that don't cost too much. You can spend all day at the leisure centre for hardly anything." **Courtney**

WHAT'S RIGHT FOR YOU?

No matter what your friends do, there are times when you've got to do what's right for you. It can be hard to do this because you don't want to fall out with your friends or miss some fun. Having more freedom also means more independence. You can make decisions that suit you, not your friends.

Getting on with the neighbours

Your first experience of independence is when you're allowed to play near your home. But this is also a test to see if you can do the right thing. Playing near your home means getting along with the neighbours and others who live close by.

Look at these photographs. Which show kids being courteous, careful and respectful?

Stepping aside?

Dropping litter?

Carrying shopping?

Making rude faces?

Can you think of times when you've been a good neighbour, or even a bad one?

A-mazing!

Work your way through the neighbourhood maze, answering each question yes or no, to see if you're a good or bad neighbour.

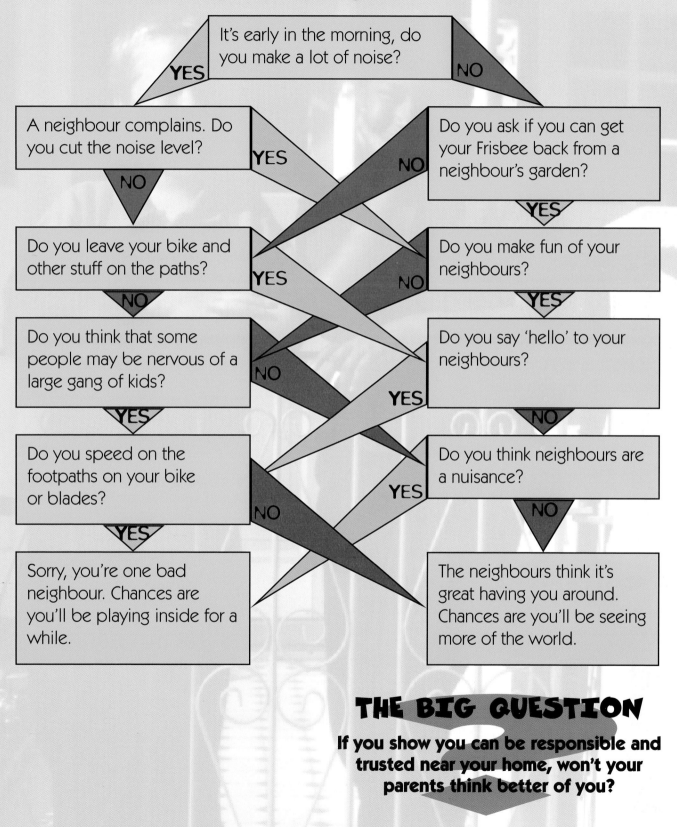

It's early in the morning, do you make a lot of noise?

YES

NO

A neighbour complains. Do you cut the noise level?

Do you ask if you can get your Frisbee back from a neighbour's garden?

YES

NO

NO

YES

Do you leave your bike and other stuff on the paths?

Do you make fun of your neighbours?

YES

NO

NO

YES

Do you think that some people may be nervous of a large gang of kids?

Do you say 'hello' to your neighbours?

NO

YES

YES

NO

Do you speed on the footpaths on your bike or blades?

Do you think neighbours are a nuisance?

NO

YES

YES

NO

Sorry, you're one bad neighbour. Chances are you'll be playing inside for a while.

The neighbours think it's great having you around. Chances are you'll be seeing more of the world.

THE BIG QUESTION

If you show you can be responsible and trusted near your home, won't your parents think better of you?

WHEELY GOOD TIMES

There's nothing better than being able to get around on your bike, blades or skateboard and having a great time. The problem is there's not always a special place where you can 'chuck wheelies', or 'grind and ollie', so you have to use footpaths and other safe public areas. Here, you may have to mix in with pedestrians.

How road-smart are you? Crash hot or not? Try this quiz to find out.

1 Are bicycles allowed on footpaths?

a) No, only if there is a marked cycle path.
b) Who cares? I'll cycle where I want!
c) Don't know.

2 You're on your blades, going real fast and coming to a corner. Do you ...

a) Slow right down – there might be something coming the other way?
b) Crouch low so that you don't lose any speed?
c) Yell "Watch out, I'm coming through!"

3 Do you wear safety gear all the time?

a) You bet. I don't want to slam and get hurt.
b) Nah, it's only for wimps.
c) Only when I think I might have an accident.

4 You're skateboarding on a footpath. Who has right of way – you or a pedestrian?

a) The pedestrian.
b) Me, 'cause I'm king of the road'.
c) Whoever's last to get out of the way.

5 You're on your skateboard and want to cross a busy road. Do you ...

a) Go to the nearest crossing, stop, get off your board and carry it across the road?
b) Speed up and dodge the cars?
c) Not notice the road at all?

6 If you're cycling on the road, do you follow the same rules as other road traffic?

a) Yes.
b) Only if there's police around.
c) What road rules?

7 It's getting dark and raining, you're not wearing fluoro-striped clothes and your bike has no lights. Do you ...

a) Get a lift home or maybe walk the bike home on the footpath?
b) Go for it. Rain won't hurt you?
c) Cycle slowly?

8 What do you think about people who hitch a tailgate ride when they're cycling, blading or boarding?

a) They are dead stupid. It's so dangerous!
b) Dead cool!
c) Dead envious because they're so brave.

HOW DID YOU GO?

All As: You're road-smart, but keep learning and brushing up your knowledge.

Anything less than all As: You're not road-smart. There are no second prizes when it comes to road safety and common sense. You're a danger to yourself and others.

GETTING ROAD-SMART

Before you even take your first bike ride or roll on your board or skates, you should know the basics of starting, stopping and road safety. Beginners can go to cycle proficiency classes and there are some great classes for learning how to blade or board. You can find out about these classes through your school; local council or leisure centre; skate park; and cycle, skate or board shop; and by checking out information in magazines or on the Internet. You may even find out useful contact numbers through your local police station. All these sports have official organizations that run classes.

AGGRESSIVE NOT AGGRO

Aggressive riding, blading and boarding where you do great tricks has nothing to do with being aggro. Aggro is when you're rude to others, buzz or scare people, or just behave in a threatening manner. The world's best aggressive riders are the best because they are road-smart, have common sense and respect for others. So don't confuse being an ace aggressive rider with being a bullying, show-off nerd.

15

MIND YOUR MANNERS

Having good manners isn't just about not slurping your soup, eating with your mouth closed and saying 'please' and 'thank you'. Good manners, in other words – being polite and courteous, come in handy just about everywhere and in every situation.

When Cathy was invited to stay overnight at Michelle's house, she packed everything but her manners.

CATHY, GO HOME!

> Would you like another sandwich, Cathy?
>
> No.

> Cath, let's help clean up.
>
> Yeh, let me finish reading this first.

> Mum, can we go to Jane's?
>
> OK, but be back by 6 o'clock.
>
> More like 10 o'clock if I've got anything to do with it!

What's Cathy done wrong?
Has she shown any respect and courtesy?
How do you think Michelle feels?
Do you think Cathy will be welcomed at Michelle's again?

STREET MANNERS

Being polite and courteous is not just about making a good impression on a friend's parent. Bad manners have consequences. How do these things affect everyone?

• Putting muddy feet on a chair.

• Dropping chewing gum on the ground.

• Not poop-scooping after your dog has fouled the footpath.

• Pushing and shoving in a bus queue.

• Using bad language.

• Not putting litter in a bin.

Sometimes adults forget to pack their manners. Some adults wrongly think that they can be rude to kids or not show them any respect. If this happens to you, don't be rude in return. Instead, be polite and courteous. Chances are, the adult will be embarrassed into making an apology.

THE BIG QUESTION

Do you think that being polite means you're a 'goody-goody', and being rude makes you 'tough'?

I was so embarrassed!

The first time you do anything new, it can be embarrassing. You worry that you'll say something stupid, or do the wrong thing or make a fool of yourself. You may even be worried that you're wearing the wrong sort of clothes. Don't worry, you're not alone – everyone feels the same.

LAUGH AND LEARN

We all make mistakes and we all take turns doing goofy things. But going into a mega-sulk and hiding in your room is not the way to handle it. Instead, have a chuckle and learn from your mistakes. No one's perfect!

"Once my skirt got caught in a revolving door in the library. When someone tried to push the door, it pulled my skirt above my knickers."
Sondra

"I got separated from my Dad at the zoo. This zoo warden asked if I needed any help, but I just shook my head. Instead, I just stood there, trying to hide the tears." **Philip**

"The first time I caught a bus by myself, I dropped my money and it rolled out of the door. Then I tripped and fell into a lady's lap. It was so embarrassing."
Sapphira

"When I first started buying stuff for myself I would only buy things that I knew the price of. I used to get all tongue-tied speaking to the sales people."
Adam

"I once went to this skating party at a leisure centre, but I was too shy to ask where the toilets were."
Jeannine

IT'S GOOD TO TALK

Do you remember the first time you met your best friend? Chances are you were both a little shy and talking didn't come easily. Now, of course, you don't stop talking. All it took was a little confidence and trust. And that's all you need when it comes to shopping by yourself or asking for help, directions or information.

This is all it takes to make a conversation:

1. Remember that what you've got to say is important and that people want to hear it.

2. Smile.

3. Look at who you're talking to. Not much use talking to your shoes.

4. Be polite and courteous.

5. Listen.

Sometimes adults talk down to kids or are rude and short-tempered with them. Don't copy what they do. Finish your conversation with them politely and then walk away. If a shopkeeper, for example, is rude to you then make a point of never going into their shop again.

THE BIG QUESTION

Now that you've got the gift of the gab, does that mean you'll be talking to everyone, including strangers?

Feeling under pressure

As you get more freedom, it's easier for so-called 'friends' to ask you to do things. They might want you to do something ...
- **that means breaking your family's rules**
- **that you don't want to do**
- **that's dangerous**
- **that's illegal**
- **that may hurt someone else**

When someone tries to make you do something you don't want to do, it's called peer pressure.

These are some of the things that you might be pressured into doing.

Skiving off school • Shoplifting • Lying • Using things like cigarettes, alcohol or illegal drugs • Buying things that are illegal for your age • Throwing things onto busy roads • Joy-riding • Mucking around on railway lines and building sites • Shouting abuse and being rude to strangers • Trespassing on private property and doing damage • Playing hurtful jokes • Stealing

Would you do any of these by yourself?

Would you do them because your friends asked you to?

What happens to kids who do these things?

Do your actions affect other people?

Rebecca's dilemma

Are these really Rebecca's friends?

Do good friends get you involved in trouble?

Getting caught is the result of doing illegal or wrong things. But why shouldn't you do wrong, illegal or dangerous things?

21

KEEP AWAY!
DANGER
ZONES!

All kids love having adventures and playing exciting games. Going to new places and trying new things is all part of growing up and seeing what the world has to offer. But some places and some things are simply dangerous. There's nothing exciting about hurting yourself or others.

Here are some dangerous places that you might want to keep clear of:

RAILWAY TRACKS

BUSY ROADS

BUILDING SITES

DANGER SLURRY PONDS

SLURRY PITS

Can you think of other dangerous places? Here's a start:

- Mining site
- Iced river
- Deserted buildings
- Refuse dump
- Electrical sub-station
- Drain tunnel

IT WON'T HAPPEN TO ME!

Lots of kids think that accidents happen to other people, not them. They are so wrong as these kids found out.

"Me and Oz ended up in hospital after mucking around in a scrap yard. We were walking on this metal pipe when it rolled away from under us. I got a broken arm and Oz had really serious concussion. We'll never be so stupid again."
Woodie

"Some friends and I took a forbidden short-cut through some waste ground. Then these older kids hassled and threatened us. We all ran in different directions to get away. I lost my way and was found miles away by the police. I still have nightmares about it."
Sue

"I was playing 'dares' at the intersection by pretending to step off the kerb and make the cars stop. I did it this one time and caused an accident. No one got hurt, but the drivers went berserk. They phoned my Mum and Dad, my school, the police, everyone."
'Grounded Forever' Marcus

What did Woodie, Sue, 'Grounded Forever' Marcus and Dave learn from their bad experiences?

What's the worst experience you've ever had? Could it have been prevented? Did you learn anything?

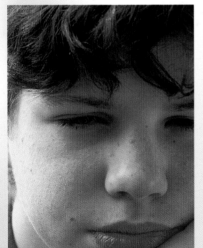

"I was just having some fun. How was I to know that Imran couldn't swim? I thought everyone could. I pushed him in, but it was his fault really."
Dave

WARNING!
Don't put yourself in danger trying to save someone from hurting themselves. The best thing you can do is get help immediately.

THE BIG QUESTION
If you saw some kids in a danger zone, what would you do?

THE FUN ZONES

Having a great time doesn't mean having a dangerous time. Here are seven cool things to do alone or with your friends when you're near home or out and about.

1. SHOW A LITTLE TENDERNESS

Getting to know people is sometimes hard, but it's dead easy to show concern, kindness and respect. Opening the door for someone pushing a pram or carrying loads of shopping costs nothing, but earns you much respect. Saying hello to your neighbours or to elderly folks also works a treat and makes you feel really good!

2. BE A FRIEND OF THE EARTH

Be aware of your environment whether it's outside your home or outside the fast-food take-way shop. Start a campaign to get better bins installed or encourage your friends not to litter.

3. EARN SOME POCKET MONEY

Hanging around is very boring, so why not turn spare time into spare cash? You could (after you've asked a parent's permission) walk someone's dog, offer to rake up leaves, wash a car, water a garden, baby-sit plants and goldfish for people on holidays, collect newspapers for recycling, help a busy parent, or do errands for elderly neighbours.

4. BE INVENTIVE

Some of the best games to play are those you and your friends have made up. You can create games that will include all your friends, and suit the location you've got. And because you invented the game, you also invent the rules!

5. GET SOMETHING STARTED

Neighbours complaining about you and your friends haring around the place on blades? Tired of not having somewhere safe to ride your bikes? Then, it's time you took some action. Get a petition going to urge the local council to provide some amenities for kids, or to encourage a leisure centre to start, say, a street hockey league. Get parents and adults involved, too.

6. HAVE A PLAN

Fun as it can be just to chill out and gossip with your friends, it's good to do other stuff. Get together with your friends, say at the beginning of the holidays, and get everyone to say what they'd like to do. It can be anything from baking biscuits and flying kites to sleepover parties and kick-boxing classes. Then work out when you can do what and plan it!

7. FIND LIKE-MINDED BODS

It's great to do some things by yourself, but some hobbies and sports call for team action. Get together with friends and start a basketball team, dare-devil skating troupe or synchronized swimming team. If your friends don't share your interests, then contact a leisure centre to see if they can help you find some like-minded spirits.

What if something happens?

Accidents happen no matter how careful you are, and sometimes even the best worked-out plans come unstuck. Here's what you should do so that a small hitch doesn't become a crisis.

You get separated from a parent or your friends

In familiar places, you can arrange to meet a parent or your friends at a particular place. This is harder to do if you're somewhere new. The best plan is to stay where you are or somewhere close and safe. Don't wander around trying to find them. It's easier for them to retrace their steps than for you to work out which way they've gone. If they don't return soon, ask a responsible adult to find you (never go with them) a police officer or someone in charge.

You get lost

Don't wander around aimlessly trying to find where you are; go to a shop or ask a responsible adult to give you directions. It's at times like this when it's important to know an exact address and a telephone number. If you're wildly lost, find the nearest phone and phone home. You have got change for the phone, yes?

You miss your train or bus

Quickly check the time of the next train or bus, then phone a parent to let them know what's happened. Don't panic and catch the next train or bus that comes – you could end up anywhere! Don't just start walking – no-one will know where you are.

You lose your money

Head towards the nearest shop, bank, post office, doctor's or dentist's surgery, police station or public building (like a library), and tell them what's happened. Ask if you can use a phone to call a parent, or if they would phone on your behalf.

You're being hassled

Don't fight or answer back. Walk quickly and immediately into a shop or other safe place where there are lots of people and explain what's happened. Don't wander around alone or in quiet areas. Phone home and arrange to be collected.

There's an accident

In case you're involved in an accident, it's important that you carry an ID card with your name, address, phone number and medical information on it. If a friend you're with has an accident, make sure someone has called for the police or an ambulance. Next thing is to contact all the parents. This is something that the police will do for you.

STRANGER DANGER

Normally you would never speak to a stranger, but in an emergency you may have no other choice. The best people to approach, if police or others in responsible positions are not around, are family groups. Be careful approaching older people, you may make them anxious.

Never go anywhere with someone you don't know at any time!

The **big** quiz

Work your way through this mega-multiple choice to see if you are road-smart, street-wise and absolutely loaded with common sense.

1. You're running late for school and there's a detention looming. Do you ...
a) Run all the way, including across the roads?
b) Walk as quickly as possible and take care crossing the roads, realizing that it's better to be late than never make it?
c) Take the short-cut through the landfill site and over the railway tracks?

2. You go shopping with a friend. You're having a great time and want to shop a bit longer. What do you do?
a) Phone home immediately.
b) Head for the nearest music shop and hang out listening to CDs.
c) Wait until your parents start to worry, then phone home.

3. You've come home and there's no one to let you in. What do you do?
a) Just hang around.
b) Go for a walk and maybe see a friend.
c) Leave a note saying where you'll be and a telephone number.

4. It's getting dark and it starts to rain, do you race inside leaving your bike, skates and junk all over a footpath?
a) Yeh, and you go inside and stay there. It's too horrible to go outside again.
b) No, you get some waterproofs on, tell an adult what you're doing and clear the path so it's safe and your gear is safe.
c) Yes, but you'll clear it after you've watched a bit of television.

5. The brakes on your bike don't work, neither do the lights. Are you going cycling with your mates?
a) Yes, it'll be alright.
b) Yeh, once everything's fixed.
c) No, don't know how to fix these things.

6. You're invited to a party. Your friend tells your parents that it's being supervised by her Mum. When you get to the party, you find her Mum's gone out. What do you do?

a) Double check and then quietly phone your parents to let them know.

b) Think this is great – no fuddy-duddy adults to ruin the fun.

c) Say nothing to your parents.

7. You're in the park with a friend when he falls from the slide. He doesn't move and his breathing is funny. What do you do?

a) Without moving him, you cover your friend with a jacket to keep him warm, then run to get help. When you return, you talk to him until help arrives.

b) Panic and run home, frightened that it's all your fault.

c) Try to pick him up and carry him to help.

8. The family next door have a baby that's only a few days old. What do you do?

a) Send a card and then make sure you keep the noise down.

b) Wish they'd stop the baby crying.

c) Same as usual – play your music and tear up and down outside their house with your mates.

9. Some kids want you to go with them to the quarry. You say you don't want to go, but your friends start to call you names. What do you do?

a) Give in and go with them.

b) Call them names in return and not change your mind.

c) Say 'bye' and then walk away.

10. What's your idea of a good day out?

a) Larking around the neighbourhood causing a bit of mischief and having some laughs.

b) Having an adventure doing some stuff that would terrify your parents.

c) You know there's loads of things that are fun to do, but that none of it is fun if something goes wrong.

Your scores

	a		b		c	
1	a	0	b	2	c	0
2	a	2	b	0	c	1
3	a	1	b	0	c	2
4	a	0	b	2	c	0
5	a	0	b	2	c	0
6	a	2	b	0	c	0
7	a	2	b	0	c	0
8	a	2	b	0	c	0
9	a	0	b	1	c	2
10	a	0	b	0	c	2

0–10 You're a danger to yourself and maybe others. Take things slower and think about what might happen.

11–15 You're pretty clued-up, but sometimes you leave your common sense at home. Pack it the next time you go out.

16–20 You're one road-smart, street-wise kid with common sense a-plenty. Keep it up.

Glossary

Bullying Teasing, frightening, threatening or hurting someone. Often done by a gang or group of kids who pick on one person.

Common sense All about thinking before doing, so that you know the consequences of your actions. If you've common sense, then you choose the safest action. If you've common sense, then you're street smart.

Communicating Being able to express your needs to others so that they understand you.

Consideration Knowing how your actions will affect others, and then behaving in a way that shows consideration.

Discrimination Treating someone differently to everyone else because of what they look like, what they wear, what they do, where they live or what they believe.

Friendship A relationship between people that is based on trust, honesty and caring.

Gang A group of children. One type of gang gets along with everyone and enjoys being together. The other sort seem set on throwing their weight around and causing trouble.

Independent Being able to do things for yourself and having your own thoughts and ideas.

Maturity There are physical changes that make your body mature, and mark your development from child to adult. Acting in a 'mature way' is when you behave, make decisions and have ideas that are grown-up.

Peer pressure When children of your own age try to make you do something that you don't want to do. They may tease you, call you names or give you the cold shoulder until you do as they want.

Books to read

Friends or Enemies? by Anita Naik (Hodder, 1997)
Stand Up For Yourself by Helen Benedict (Hodder, 1997)
Stories To Make You Think by Heather Butler (Barnabas, 1999)
What's Happening? Bullying by Karen Bryant-Mole (Wayland, 1995)
Wise Guides: Drugs by Anita Naik (Hodder, 1997/1998)

Help and advice

Many organizations like the police, education authorities, and child welfare groups produce safety brochures covering all sorts of situations, for example Stranger Danger. You can obtain these brochures through your school, local police headquarters, or by contacting the Royal Society for the Prevention of Accidents (RoSPA) at Edgbaston Park, 353 Bristol Road, Birmingham BS5 7ST, or Kidscape at 152 Buckingham Palace Road, London SW1W 9TR or call 0207 730 3300. You may also find a range of informative leaflets in your library or doctor's surgery.

If you have problems at home or at school, with your family or with friends, or just need to share your worries, talk to an adult you trust. It could be a family member or relative, a friend's parents, school nurse or counsellor, your doctor or religious leader. If you would like to talk to someone who does not know you or your family, call Childline (UK) on 0800 1111. Their telephone service is open 24-hours-a-day, the call is free and won't be listed on a telephone bill.

For information about smoking, alcohol or other drugs call National Drugs Helpline on 0800 776600. This call is free and confidential.

If you need emergency help – for example, if there's been an accident or you are in danger – call 999. This one number will give you access to the police, fire brigade and ambulance. Even though you may be frightened or anxious, speak clearly and give precise details of your name, where you are and what has happened. Don't hang up until the emergency service operator tells you to. Do not make prank calls to 999 – it could cost someone else their life! A call to 999 is free.

Picture acknowledgements
All pictures belong to the Wayland Picture Library except Bubbles 23 (top middle and bottom left) by Jennie Woodcock.

Index

accidents 23, 26, 27

choice 4, 5, 27
cinema 8-9, 11
classes 15
confidence 19
conversation 19
cultural background 10

danger 15, 22-3, 24
decision 5, 11

embarrassment 18
environment 24

fears 6
freedom 10, 11
friends 4-5, 7-8, 10-11,
  16-17,20, 26

help 23
home 12

independence 6, 11-12

lies 8
local council 15, 25

manners 16-17

neighbours 12-13, 24-5

organization 8

parents 4-5, 7-8, 10, 26
pedestrians 14
peer pressure 10, 20, 21
plan 8, 25, 26
pocket money 24

religion 11
respect 12, 17
responsibility 5, 6, 7
road safety 4-5
rules 6, 7

stealing 19, 27
strangers 19, 27